The smart Brain Train

HOW TO KEEP YOUR BRAIN HEALTHY AND WISE

by
Nina Anderson *and* Frances Meiser
in cooperation with
Susan Lee

Illustrated by
Scott Johnstone

Edu-Enviro/Health Series

Books that provide a shared experience
for children and their parents or teachers.

The Smart Brain Train

ISBN 1-884820-87-5
978-1-884820-87-8
Library of Congress Catalog Card Number 2007907239
Printed in the United States

The concepts, techniques and methods discussed in *The Smart Brain Train* are not intended as medical advice, but as suggested complementary therapeutic regimens to be considered only if deemed adequate by both patients and their chosen health professionals.

Safe Goods
561 Shunpike Rd.
Sheffield, MA 01257
413-229-7935
www.safegoodspub.com

printed on recycled paper

This book is dedicated to my nephew Bryan whose struggle has enlightened me and humbled us all.

-Frances Meiser

Hang in their bud –
You are an inspiration!

This is an Engine.

Your brain is your engine! Let's see how you can keep your engine fired up.

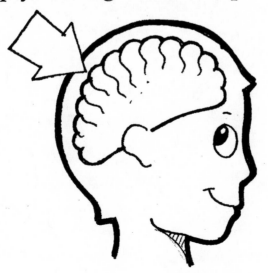

In order to keep

your engine fired up,

you need to..............

★ Drink lots of clean water!*

WHY?

Because your brain is 75% water and you need to fill it up daily...

so drink 8 BIG glasses a day !

By the way — clean water means that the bad chemicals and pesticides are taken out by running tap water through a filter. This also takes out the electrolytes which are important to your brain so you have to add them back in by drinking unsweetened sports drinks or using an electrolyte supplement that you add to water.

You also need to eat plenty of brain food.*

*Your brain is hungry for energy and needs it more than any other part of your body.

Brain foods are:

<u>WHOLE GRAINS</u>
like rye, millet, brown rice,
oats, whole wheat.
(*but not white rice or white bread*)

<u>MEAT, NUTS and SEEDS</u>
like chicken, fish, lentils,
pumpkin seeds, eggs, walnuts, almonds,
sunflower seeds, and sprouts.

<u>VEGETABLES and FRUIT</u>
like green beans, carrots, spinach, broccoli,
spring salad greens, sweet potatoes,
bananas, blueberries, apples, grapes
and strawberries.

and

<u>OILS and FLAX</u>

Flax seeds are hard, shiny, brown and gold and look kind of like birdseed.

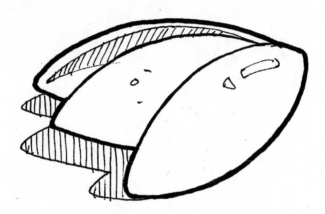

They come from a pretty purple flower and taste yummy like nuts. Flax seeds are tasty when ground up and sprinkled on your cereal or put into pancakes or muffins.

Flax makes fat nerve fibers. This helps your brain work faster than with skinny fibers, so you can think more quickly!

In addition to flax, oils like borage, olive, primrose and walnut can help brain cells absorb oxygen and keep them healthy and happy.

This helps your brain work better!*

If you want your engine to run at full speed, you need to keep the left side and the right side of your brain connected.

To do this you need...........................

Movement, and lots of it!

Movement is important to keep both sides of your brain working together. As we move and cross our midline (a line drawn from your chin to your belly button)...

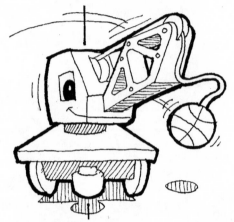

the right and left sides of our brain begin to work together.

★ Activities like this are good.

The right brain is our visual side.
It sees the whole picture.

The left brain sees only little bits
and pieces of the picture.

Therefore, it is important to exercise both
sides of your brain through the crossing
movements.

Last but not least...

Did you know that your reading skills start when you are a baby?

When you crawl, suck on something or roll over a lot, you prepare your brain for reading.

These are movements that cross the midline and exercise your brain.

Now that you're bigger you can do other simple things to help your brain...........➜

Did you ever drink through one of those crazy straws?

It sounds weird, but this kind of straw actually:

➡ helps both sides of your brain to work together,

➡ helps your brain learn words,

➡ helps your eyes to focus.

Playing electronic games can help you improve your brain's speed and memory, but don't forget to go outside and play.

Exercises are good, too – your brain
gets a real work out keeping all
those muscles working at the right time!

You must never forget that your brain is your engine ...

and **YOU** are responsible for keeping it fired up!

Have fun and use your personal chart on the next page to record what you do each day. This will help you keep your brain train chugging in tip-top shape.

MY PROGRESS CHART

	MON	TUE	WED	THU	FRI	SAT	SUN
I fed my brain:							
Nuts							
Protein							
Grains							
Flax and oils							
Glasses of water with electrolytes I drank today (8 is best!)							
Did I exercise today?							
My midline was crossed how many times?							

Remember...

A healthy brain can make learning fun!

Keep up your chart and your engine will
be happy.

Make learning easy and fun!

Supplemental Information
for Parents and Teachers

It is estimated that 15-20% of students in every classroom are not achieving grade levels as well as they could. Some may have been labeled Learning Disabled (LD); Attention Deficit Disorder (ADD); Attention Deficit Hyperactive Disorder (ADHD), Dyslexia or others. Even a child who hasn't been diagnosed may be experiencing a more difficult time in school. Neurological immaturity is often the cause of these learning difficulties wherein the messages are not properly being transmitted and received in the brain. Brain connections are normally developed during our baby and toddler years. This is why it is so important to start your child early on a pathway to brain health. By taking an active roll in the child's brain development you may help him/her to achieve high levels of learning with fewer roadblocks.

This section is provided for educators and moms and dads to help in understanding the parameters behind healthy brain development and sustenance. Not only is the information pertinent to children, but grown-ups can benefit as well. For an adult version read *Overcoming Senior Moments* (see other books by Safe Goods at the end of this book). Expanded information is formatted as it appears in the illustrated pages.

The Brain

The brain is a flurry of electrical transmissions caused by signaling mechanisms called neurotransmitters. This is the chemical language sent between cells in the human brain. These neurotransmitters allow the brain cells to talk to each other. Deficiency in neuro-transmitter function results in depression, lifelessness, moods, irritability, sleeplessness, anxiety, brain fog, cravings and addictions. Depleted supplies of the "feel good" neurotransmitters make it difficult for you to feel happy, on track and motivated. Neuro-transmitter deficiencies can be caused by genetics, stress, diets low in amino acids, and through alcohol or drug abuse. Neurotransmitter support is necessary for the brain to function at top performance. Memory loss may be nothing more than an amino acid (protein) deficiency, causing a short circuit. No matter what we do, our thinking process determines the outcome of our actions.

Information in the brain is processed when the incoming signal from receptor goes to the dendrite and into the neuron. The neuron transmits down the axon then dispenses information through chemical neurotransmitters to other cells receptors. Without proper chemical neurotransmitters an erroneous signal or no signal is sent (see diagram at right).

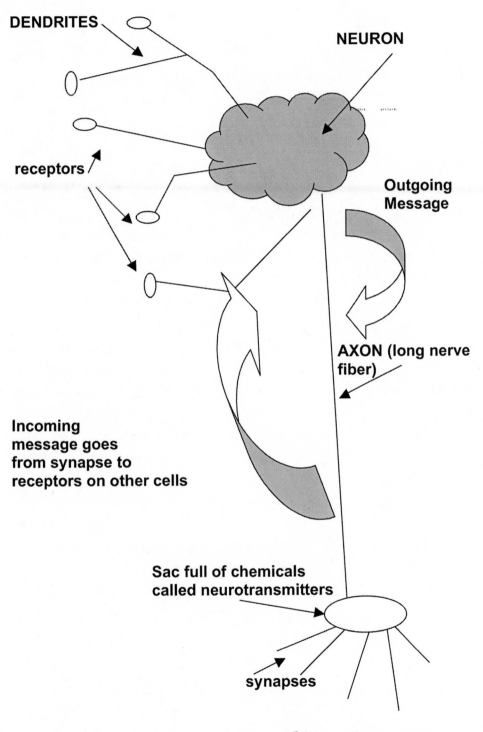

DENDRITES

NEURON

receptors

Outgoing
Message

**AXON (long nerve
fiber)**

Incoming
message goes
from synapse to
receptors on other cells

Sac full of chemicals
called neurotransmitters

synapses

23

Water

Water is life. The number one ingredient for brain health is so simple that most of us forget it. Water is life. Since the brain is 75 percent water, it is logical to assume that low water content will affect cognitive function and neurotransmitter function. That's why we suggest eight glasses of water a day. Many of us get busy and forget to drink water, or prefer something sweeter like carbonated drinks or juice. Although these substitutes do contain water, they also are considered food because of ingredients that need to be digested. This means that not all of the water goes to places in the body where it needs to be.

When we speak about drinking lots of water, we caution you to qualify what is in the water. Spring water is the best, but unfortunately very few of us may live near a mountain brook. If you are on a city water system, chances are your water has most likely been treated with chlorine to kill bacteria. Unfortunately, when this chlorine meets decaying plant matter (like in your intestines), it can form Trihalomethanes, which are known to cause cancer. Fluoride also is put into city water. In small quantities this helps teeth, but too much fluoride can actually cause mottling of the teeth. It is important that if your tap water comes from a city water system that you consider purchasing a water filter. Countertop models are convenient and can do a great job of filtering out the harmful stuff. Bottled water is better than unfiltered tap water, but if stored for a long time (as in the store), can actually grow bacteria. Well water is okay as long as you have it tested once in awhile for bacteria and heavy metals.

Most of the water we get for drinking today is deficient in trace minerals. Unless you drink from a mountain stream, chances are that the water has lost its minerals on the trip from the reservoir to your tap. Since purified water (bottled water and filtered tap water) also has many of the essential trace minerals removed, it is necessary to put them back in yourself. Minerals can best be added to the water by using a liquid supplement in a crystalloid form (the smallest form of mineral). Next best are ionic and/or chelated minerals. Colloidal minerals are usually too large to squeeze into your cells and therefore should be your last choice for supplementation. Ionic trace minerals are highly absorbable and are a good choice.

Minerals in the brain create the necessary spark. Called electrolytes, these charged particles are responsible for signals being delivered from one cell to the other. Salmon swimming upstream, when confronted with a waterfall, swim in circles at the base of the falling water. This helps them absorb the electrical charge created by the falling water, ultimately facilitating their miraculous climb up the waterfall. If electrolytes can do this for a fish, just think what they can do for your brain. On the other hand, if you are mineral deficient, the brain cannot create sparks and eventually short circuits. This can definitely hamper your ability to remember anything and everything.

Only certain minerals form these electrolytes. Electrolytes are needed to keep the body's balance of fluids at the proper level and to maintain normal functions, such as heart rhythm, muscle contraction, and brain function. Most sports drinks contain sodium and potassium. Unfortunately these don't really form electrolytes even though the word electrolyte is used by their manufacturers. You must have more than just two minerals to make electrolytes. In addition, the formula should include boron, which is a carrier into the cell. Most sports drinks also contain sugar, artificial sweeteners, dyes and high levels of sodium that could be dangerous to children if they drink more than a serving per day. These sweet drinks promoted as sports drinks usually contain so many calories that drinking them can contribute to obesity and we are seeing more and more overweight kids today.

Both children and adults can benefit from regular use of an electrolyte drink. When we rehydrate with water alone that does not contain electrolytes we may be asking for trouble. The blood needs minerals to create electrolytes and if it can't get them from the water it starts asking the bones to give up some. This causes bone loss, and in children can make them more susceptible to breaks, especially during sports activities. Drinking too much mineral-deficient water can actually cause a condition where the electrolytes are flushed from the brain and the heart cannot function. Marathon runners have fallen victim to this malady and have died, so it is extremely important to find out what kind of water you are drinking – even if you have to ask the manufacturer. Water is life, but water without electrolytes can have detrimental effects on the body.

Brain Food

Nutrient support is necessary to keep our neuro-transmitters operational. Foods that support brain health include: (a) vegetable protein such as fermented soy, sea vegetables and beans; (b) whole grains (rye, millet, whole wheat, spelt, brown rice); (c) fresh fruit with an emphasis on unsprayed organic varieties; vegetables (preferably organic) like cauliflower, broccoli and spinach which induce a calming effect due to their high calcium and/or L-tryptophan content; (d) nuts, seeds, nuts, fish, and d) bananas which all help to reduce stress because of their high vitamin B content. Avoid junk food, fast food, and ingredients like BHA, BHT, artificial sweeteners, nitrates or food coloring.

The U.S. Food and Drug Administration seems to be quick to approve food additives, and reluctant to take them out even after mountains of proof have shown that they create illness and even death. One of these which has been studied at length is Aspartame, the sugar-substitute. Used in diet foods, children's electrolyte formulas and drinks, this additive is now thought to create a craving for carbo-hydrates and may not really be for dieters at all. At the World Environmental Conference in 1997, it was disclosed that when the temperature of Aspartame exceeds 86 degrees F, the wood alcohol in it converts to formaldehyde and then to formic acid (the poison found in the sting of fire ants), which in turn causes metabolic acidosis. As far as brain health goes, memory loss attributed to aspartame ingestion is due to the fact that aspartic acid and phenylalanine (what makes up aspartame) are neurotoxic without the other amino acids found in protein. Thus it goes past the blood brain barrier and deteriorates the neurons of the brain. Aspartame also comes with a list of side effects that includes seizures, nausea, depression, migraine headaches, numbness, blindness and potentially detrimental affect on the brain's neuro-transmitters. Scientific studies performed on Aspartame to establish its safety prior to FDA approval, revealed brain tumors and grand mal seizures in rats. We recommend not allowing children to eat and drink aspartame.

Other artificial sweeteners commonly used may also affect children's health: Acesulfame K (causes cancer in animals), sucralose (animal studies have revealed negative effects on the thymus gland, enlarged liver and kidneys, decreased red blood cell count and diarrhea), and high fructose corn syrup (linked to irritable bowel syndrome and obesity). Sugar is probably the safest sweetener but it can increase hyperactivity and temporarily reduce concentration. However, it is a better alternative than artificial sweeteners unless too much is eaten. Sugarholics can "get the *sugar dumbs*" according to Sabina Wise in her book, *The Sugar Addict's Diet*. In maintaining the blood sugar balance, which has been upset by a constant infusion of sugar, the brain takes a direct hit. Low blood sugar symptoms can appear within twenty minutes of eating sugar and result in mental and emotional disturbances as well as short-term memory problems."

Foods that can affect brain function by creating allergic responses in children are corn, wheat, milk and chocolate. These may result in symptoms of fatigue, lack of concentration, irritability and lethargy. Not all kids respond to food allergies, but, should a symptom arise, this factor must be taken into consideration. If we expect children to develop healthy brains and healthy bodies, we must take into consideration what they are putting in their mouths. If you feed them meat, poultry or fish, vegetables, some starches, a wee bit of sugar and lots of water you will have far smarter children than if they eat junk food, soda pop, candy and processed foods.

Another widely accepted food is soy but it can affect brain function negatively when not taken in the proper form. Parents who give children soy rather than milk may have made a poor choice. Rich in phytonutrients, soy is most beneficial when eaten in a fermented or sprouted form. Raw soybeans, and foods made from them may have difficulty being digested because of a trypsin enzyme inhibitor, and therefore their nutrients may not be available to the body. Soy formula may be in this category. Recently, certain soy products have been suspected in causing memory loss and brain damage in men and unborn children.[1] Normally made from unsprouted soy, most soy products have difficulty in being digested through the normal enzymatic process. The body in its effort to rid itself of this food uses minerals as carriers for the elimination process. If enough unfermented soy is eaten, this will reduce the mineral levels in the body. This may actually affect the brain, because as we have stated before, minerals are essential for proper brain function.

---

[1] Barnett, Antony, "Soya alert over cancer and brain damage link," *Guardian Newspapers Ltd.*, (www.observer.co.uk) August, 2000

Essential Fatty Acids (good fats)

The brain is structurally composed of 60 percent fat, so it makes sense that fats are critical to brain health. Fat supports protection for the myelin sheath that surrounds the nerve fibers in the brain. If compromised, this covering will no longer provide protection against short circuits, resulting in memory loss. Cells in the body need oxygen. The brain needs oxygen. The body requires special fats that among other important functions make it possible for sufficient oxygen to reach the cells via the cell membranes. These special fats are highly oxygen-absorbing entities called essential fatty acids (EFAs) and must be consumed daily since the body can't manufacture them. Flax is a great brain food. Adding olive oil, Borage, evening primrose and black currant oils together can provide the proper balance of omega-3 and omega-6 essential fatty acids. But, most people are not chemists and do not know how much of all of these oils to take. In addition, we need to take "parent" EFAs – omega 6 linoleic acid (LA) and omega 3 alpha-linolenic acid (ALA). These parent EFAs (not derived such as GLA) affect the permeability of cell membranes, making them much more able to absorb oxygen. If we are EFA deficient, we may inhibit the cellular absorption of oxygen thereby diminishing brain function. Brian Peskin, BSEE also has done studies revealing an oxygen-rich cell is highly resistant to cancer.

Foods rich in omega-3 are flax, animal foods and fish. Eating these without foods containing omega-6 such as oils, nuts and seeds can unbalance the body. Warnings about consuming too much omega-6 have people bulking up on omega-3. Unfortunately, most of those warnings are targeting the hydrogenated oils that convert to trans fatty acids and are the subject of many articles linking them to clogged arteries. Eating unprocessed organic oils that contain the parent Omega-6 in a proper ratio with omega-3's is advised by Peskin. If you are confused as to how to do this, he has produced a supplement that you can take to assure you are getting the right amount of EFAs. (see Resource Directory).

There is also a fat, a phospholipid called Physphatidylserine (PS), that is found throughout the body but is concentrated in the inside layer of brain cell membranes. This membrane provides structural support and helps keep cell membranes fluid and flexible; but most importantly, it is involved in the transmissions of information across the synaptic gap between cells. PS enhances the activity of receptors in the brain cells' membrane and boosts the synthesis and release of certain neurotransmitters that pass messages from one brain cell to another. Although our bodies produce PS they manufacture less of this substance, as we grow older. We can obtain PS from dark green vegetables but since we normally don't eat enough of these taking a supplement may be a feasible alternative. Young children don't have to worry too much about a lack of PS but adults, especially those middle-aged or older should, which is why we mention it in this section tailored for grown-ups. Supplemental PS may benefit the brain by restoring normal levels of the brain neurotransmitter acetylcholine and by holding back the degeneration of dendrites (the part of a nerve cell that carries a nerve impulse to the cell body) in the brain's hippocampus.

Enzymes

Enzymes are necessary to break down the good fats. Since most of us eat cooked foods, we are enzyme deficient. Many of the enzymes occurring naturally in raw food are killed during the heating process. Your body must now depend on the pancreas to produce the needed enzymes. Eventually this organ gets tired and produces less and less enzymes, leading to undigested foods and the diseases associated with maldigestion which include allergies, fatigue, and lethargy. Lipase is the enzyme needed to break down fats, therefore supplementation may be necessary to enhance absorption of the good fats that support the brain. When choosing an enzyme supplement, pick one that says "plant enzymes" on the container as this type works throughout the entire digestive tract, not just in the stomach.

Movement and Brain Health

We sometimes wonder whether our child's brain is working properly. If they have difficulty learning is it because of genetics or diet or emotional problems or lack of exercise? Barbara Pheloung from Move To Learn in Manly, Australia has a list on her website (www.movetolearn.com.au) that gives you an indication of a potential learning disability. The following can be an indicator that you should look further into the behavioral problem: (a) children on the go; (b) children that are left out of activities; c) writes in mirror image; (d) clumsy; (e) dyslexic; (f) hates firecrackers; (g) puts shoes on the wrong foot; (h) extreme mood swings; (i) unable to find things; (j) poor sitting positions. While not all of these behaviors need be present, if however, you notice that your child has learning difficulties then maybe you ought to consider a brain-stimulating exercise program.

Physical movements stimulate the brain. Therefore, the more we move the smarter we become. Exercises that cross a line from head to toe right down your middle, stimulates the neurons in the brain. Neurodevelopment begins when we are babies. The first movements that cross the midline like sucking, rolling over and crawling encourage brain development. Sitting in a car seat for hours does not. As a child develops, activities that integrate the physical with the mental function can be: jumping rope, jumping on a trampoline, martial arts, skipping, walking while swinging your arms, jacks, chess, Yoga, puzzles, sweeping floors, badminton and tennis for starters. Activities that do not further development are those that require sitting for long periods of time (TV, computers).

Educational Kinesiology was developed in the early 1980's by Dr. Paul E. Dennison, who says, "We are all 'learning blocked' to the extent that we have learned not to move." His research and theories grew into a system of exercises for the brain called Brain Gym. These 23 movements are based on over 25 years of research and are endorsed by the National Learning Foundation. They build from the premise that every nerve and cell is a network contributing to our intelligence and our learning capability. Many educators have found this work quite helpful in improving overall concentration in class.

These exercises integrate the brain in various dimensions allowing information to flow easily from sense into memory and then out again. An example of an exercise is to visualize the letter X. This activates the brain for whole-body coordination and increases concentration. A few other exercises are listed below:

Brain Buttons

This exercise helps improve blood flow to the brain to "switch on" the entire brain before a lesson begins. The increased blood flow helps improve concentration skills required for reading, writing, etc.

- Put one hand so that there is as wide a space as possible between the thumb and index finger.
- Place your index and thumb into the slight indentations below the collarbone on each side of the sternum. Press lightly in a pulsing manner.
- At the same time put the other hand over the navel area of the stomach. Gently press on these points for about 2 minutes.

Cross Crawl

This exercise helps coordinate right and left brain by exercising the information flow between the two hemispheres. It is useful for spelling, writing, listening, reading and comprehension.

- Stand or sit. Put the right hand across the body to the left knee as you raise it, and then do the same thing for the left hand on the right knee just as if you were marching.
- Do this sitting or standing for about two minutes.

Hook Ups

This works well for nerves before a test or special event such as making a speech. Any situation which will cause nervousness calls for a few "hook ups" to calm the mind and improve concentration.

- Stand or sit. Cross the right leg over the left at the ankles.
- Cross the right wrist over the left wrist and link up the fingers so the right wrist is on top.
- Bend the elbows out and gently turn the fingers in towards the body until they rest on the sternum (breast bone) in the center of the chest. Stay in this position.
- Keep the ankles crossed and the wrists crossed and then breathe evenly in this position for a few minutes. You will be noticeably calmer after that time.

If you child is having learning or recall difficulties, we suggest you explore these types of exercise programs for the brain. The Brain Gym folks are listed in the Resource Directory at the end of this book.

Electronic Games

Do electronic games help children's intellectual skills or can they create problems that inhibit learning and encourage bad habits? In most respects they help develop healthy brain activity. NASA research on brain waves has instigated creation of virtual reality biofeedback using electronic games. This technique uses software that reinforces the faster brain 'beta' waves through using the joystick during a specific game to control the characters on the screen. When players use slower, more lethargic brain waves (theta waves) the game pad is sluggish, while using beta waves speeds up the pad. This type of biofeedback improved concentration.

Electronic games are also being used to study how the brain works to point to cures for both epilepsy and memory disorders. A team of neuroscientists from Brandeis University and Children's Hospital in Boston, Massachusetts, examined electrical activity in the brains of teenagers as they maneuvered through virtual mazes.[2] The key to success in the game is remembering where you've been and how you got there. Researchers focused on slow, rhythmic waves of electrical activity known as theta oscillations that are produced when groups of brain cells (neurons) all fire at once. It has been known that epileptic seizures are spurred by brain waves that go awry. Seizures usually start in a part of the brain called the temporal lobe, which plays a key role in memory. By using the electronic games to analyze how the brain remembers, researchers may be able to come up with better treatments for epilepsy.

---

[2] Brandeis University release, "Scientists at Children's Hospital and Brandeis Use Video Games to Unlock Secrets off the Brain's Sense of Direction," *Science Daily*, 6/15/1999

So you see that electronic games have mainstreamed themselves in the research arena of brain health. They also can be good tools for education, treatment of behavioral disorders, memory enhancement and they have been shown to prepare children for a fast paced business environment especially where problem solving, working with teams and analyzing risks are needed. With 90 million gamers playing, this is a big impact on society. But one downside that is being documented is addiction. "One in eight youthful gamers develop all of the patterns similar to an addiction," says Dr. David Walsh with the National Institute on Media and the Family.[3] Electronic games can also be responsible for lack of adequate exercise, fostering eyestrain and create violent behavior.

Since many of the games promote killing or vanquishing the opponent, children are more likely not to associate the actual risks of aggressive behavior that they learned in a virtual environment. When children whose minds are being formed are bombarded with negative images (killing, fighting, war) it is only reasonable to assume that they will react in a virtual way to a real situation. Killing may not, in their mind, be a bad thing with societal consequences. They may not be able to process the situation correctly. Because part of learning is repetition and, if they game enough, this negative repetitive behavior will permanently lodge in the brain and be called upon when action is needed, whether it be virtual or not. The distinction between acceptable behavior and that learned in the game may not be made. It is up to the

---

[3] Lewis, George, Correspondent NBC News, "Researchers tout positive effects of video games," May 19, 2005 www.msnbc.msn.com

parent or educator to screen the games and let their child play only those that evoke positive lifestyles.

The University of Minnesota Extension published a list of guidelines for parents to follow when choosing electronic games for their families. These are designed to maximize the positive effects of the games by creating motivation, reaping clear and quick feedback about performance and generating a feeling of mastery for their participants. Some of these guidelines include:[4]

- Select games that promote problem solving. Think about your child's needs and choose games that sharpen their capacities.
- Set limits for the amount of time your child plays alone. Examples: one hour for video, one to two hours of TV per day.
- Look for games that stress cooperation. Try not to pick ones where violence is rewarded.
- Play games with your child. This helps monitor the content and determine which games get rented.
- Use the E.S.R.B. ratings listed on the box. E is appropriate for everyone age 6 and up; T for teens 12 and up; M for mature audiences are not appropriate for youth. Most stores don't enforce these ratings so parents must be the watchdogs.
- Pay attention to the attitudes expressed toward gender roles in games. Try to select games that portray both sexes positively and include both sexes.

---

[4] Univ. of Minnesota, "Video Games: A Problem or a Blessing?"
www.extension.umn.edu/info-u/families/BE933.html

Chiropractic

Although we don't mention this in the children's section of this book we thought it was important information for parents and teachers. Surprising as it may sound, chiropractic treatment may help to increase brain function. During a lifetime we all experience falls, jarring bumps in cars and planes, twisting strains, sitting doing tasks for hours or even stressful emotional outbreaks. These episodes can cause your back or neck to get a "crook" in it. If not corrected, misalignment can develop into a chronic condition that we accept and just learn to live with.

When the vertebrae of the neck become misaligned (subluxation), it decreases the size of the holes between the vertebrae where the nerves lie. This pinching type action causes pressure on the nerves and on the blood vessels decreasing blood to the brain. According to Dr. Ogi Ressel, D.C., and author of *Kids First, Health with No Interference*, "a vertebral subluxation is an irritant to the nervous system. It is similar to having a pebble placed in your shoe that you can't get rid of." Chiropractic care is directed at correcting these subluxations. It helps the nervous system function normally, by increasing blood flow resulting in reduced brain trauma.

Children who come through the birth canal and are pulled out can have misalignments. This may be one of the root causes of learning roadblocks and chiropractic or cranial sacral therapy should be high on the list of treatment options prior to any drugs being administered. Many times children with ADD are mysteriously cured by simple chiropractic adjustment (if that was the cause of the neural breakdown). In order for your child to have the best chance at developing a healthy brain it is advised that they have a chiropractic check up if any learning disability is suspected.

Activities that may be bad for the brain

Activities that do *not* foster further development of the brain are those associated with electromagnetic energy (EMF) and radio frequencies (RF). EMFs work at different frequencies than the human body, which tries to convert them to a harmonious cycle. The effort expended in this process not only compromises the immune system, but adds stress to the brain, reducing its effectiveness. Computers (with older cathode ray tube monitors), video games, and electronic toys all provide electromagnetic frequencies that can negatively affect the user. Plasma screens are safer, but if you sit near the computer tower you still may be subjected to high levels of EMFs. For maximum protection, make sure the user sits three feet away from the television or computer (need keyboard with long cord). It is also wise to investigate the many protective devices that are sold, such as elemental diodes, and cathode ray tube shields. For further information, you can read Dr. Glen Swartwout's book, *Electromagnetic Pollution Solutions* (see bibliography).

Cellular phones are under study and early reports reveal that learning in children is impaired for up to an hour after the phone is used. University of Utah researcher Om Gandhi, found that the younger the child, the more radiation is absorbed in brain tissue, according to sources who have spoken with him. His new data is consistent with earlier work on radiation absorption. As outlined in an article in the *Journal of Cellular Biochemistry* (see bibliography) some fear children may be more susceptible to mobile-phone radiation than adults because their nervous systems are still developing. Phone headsets may offer some protection because the unit is not being placed next to the brain, but to be sure, it still may be advisable to limit usage of cell phones by children. A 2003 report from Lund University in Sweden found that rats at the development level of human teenagers experienced brain damage after being exposed to normal cell phone radiation. Wi-Fi is also undergoing health studies in foreign countries. Germany's Federal Office for Radiation Protection has recently advised that people should avoid using Wi-Fi wherever possible because of the risks it may pose to health. Florain Emrich, for the office, says Wi-Fi should be avoided, "because people receive exposures from many sources and because it is a new technology and all the research into its health effects has not yet been carried out."[5] Even Ontario, Canada's Lakehead University banned Wi-Fi on campus because of its suspected health risks. If you are concerned about WiFi you may want to encourage your child's school to postpone installation until more research into its safety has been done.

Another hazard to brain health is the frequencies coming out of cell towers that are close to your residence or your child's school. Blake Levitt in her book, *Cell Towers: Wireless Convenience or Environmental Hazard,* lists safety concerns from these towers that has spanned decades. Many schools allow cell tower construction on their campuses in exchange for the telecommunication company financially assisting with the construction of a new ball field, new gymnasium, etc. With little consideration for any potential health

---

[5] "Hold the Line: The Debate Over the Health Effects of Wireless," *Washington Post*, Sept. 9, 2007, pg N02

hazards for children, school officials eagerly welcome these towers. My foster daughter's school was the recipient of a cell tower at their school. Within two weeks after it became operational there was an increase in violence among the children, poor academic results and depression. This lasted throughout the period she attended that school (we eventually changed schools as her learning curve was so badly affected we didn't think she would ever graduate). According to Robert O. Becker, M.D., Biomedical sciences consultant and author of *Cross Currents*, "the continued proliferation of this radiation constitutes one of the most significant alterations of the natural environment, with the possibility of major impacts on human health." We would advise any parent that sees a change in their child's behavior or learning curve to examine the possibility of EMF interference including cell tower citing near the school or home. Unseen frequencies can be just as much a problem for the brain as head trauma or poor diet. It is wise for all of us to research both sides of the EMF story and decide for ourselves it this could be affecting your child's learning ability.

Resource Directory

ELECTROBLAST™ Fun for kids and a taste they will like – a liquid portable formulation of essential electrolytes that makes a great drink. A tasty way for kids (and adults) to hydrate the brain; a tasty electrolyte drink without sugar or artificial sweeteners. ELECTROBLAST™ provides 11 trace-minerals plus great natural flavor. Our 2 oz. size makes 60 drinks and saves landfill waste when used with a refillable water bottle. Easy-to-carry in lunchboxes, pockets, backpacks, and purses. ELECTROBLAST™ is the most convenient way to add minerals to your diet. LJB PIPER, LLC, P.O. Box 36, E. Canaan CT, 06024 (413) 229-9042 www.electroblast.com

LIQUID CRYSTALLOID ELECTROLYTE MINERALS. Trace-Lyte™ is a crystalloid (smallest form) electrolyte formula that helps keep cells strong, balance pH, facilitate removal of toxins and provide the body's life force. It helps maintain the body's primary bio-oxidation process and raises the Osmotic Pressure of the cell walls, strengthening them. High absorption is achieved due to its crystalloid structure. Unlike most earth-type liquid minerals, there is no heavy metal contamination. NATURE'S PATH, INC., PO box 7862, Venice, FL 34287-7862 (800)-326-5772

"NUTRI-TECH" THE ULTIMATE WATER FILTRATION SYSTEM. Pure water is an essential element for good health. Carico International has developed a "POINT OF USE" system with a unique design that has no moving parts nor requires electricity. It incorporates a multi-stage technology including sub-micron ceramic and selective adsorbents to address all priority pollutants including microorganisms. In addition, the entire system is enclosed in surgical stainless steel with a cleanable, removable cartridge. Comes with installation kit and video. CARICO INTERNATIONAL, 50 Lisbon Pl., Staten Island, NY 10306-2456 (888)-4CI-PURE (424-7873) or (718)-667-7022

DIGESTIVE ENZYMES AND EFAs. *TymeZyme™* an all-natural formula, contains all the necessary enzymes for digestion throughout the intestinal tract. It contains protease, amylase, lipase, cellulase and lactase. When taken with meals, it increases absorption and assures the body of receiving the benefits of vital nutrients, especially zinc, selenium, vitamin B6 and essential fatty acids. Enzymes also guard against maldigestion and associated food allergies, reducing their associated emotional and behavioral effects. *YES Essential Fatty Acids* have parent omega-6 and omega-3 in the proper combination to assure cellular oxygen uptake and help prevent cancer, which can't live in an oxygen rich environment. The formula takes into consideration the good "parent" omega-6 you may already be getting in your diet as well as carefully balancing it with the proper ratio of "parent" omega-3. LONG LIFE CATALOGS, PO Box 36, E. Canaan, CT 06024 www.longlifecatalogs.com 888-217-7233.

BRAIN GYM. An educational program including exercises that integrate the brain in various dimensions allowing information to flow easily from sense into memory and then out again. Edu-K is a worldwide network dedicated to enhancing living and learning through the science of movement. For more than 30 years and in over 80 countries they have been helping children, adults and seniors to improve learning, stay more focused and organized, overcome learning challenges and more. BRAIN GYM™ INTERNATIONAL, 1575 Spinnaker Dr., Ste. 204B, Ventura, CA 03001, (800)-356-2109 For books and publications visit: www.braingym.com.

The HANDLE® INSTITUTE. A thorough, yet gentle evaluation of each client's neurological function will identify root causes of a variety of learning disorders (such as ADD/ADHD, dyslexia and Tourette's Syndrome.) From this knowledge, a personalized treatment program is designed for each client for practice in the home. Programs take about 30 minutes per day and typically produce significant results within 6 weeks. The HANDLE® Institute, 1300 Dexter Avenue North 110, The Casey Family Building, Seattle, Washington 98109 (206)-860-2665 Website: www.handle.org

DAKOTA FLAX GOLD. An excellent natural source of essential fatty acids. We have fresh golden flaxseed for you. Also, we have a grinder with the package of seeds so you can grind your own flax. Seeds must be ground for full nutrition. Ground golden flax tastes excellent with milk and honey ... or for a special treat, put seeds on frozen pizza, then bake. Send self-addressed stamped envelope (SASE) for free sample so you can taste how good these seeds really are. HEINTZMAN FARMS, RR 2 Box 265, Onaka SD 57466 (800)-333-5813 Website: www.heintzmanfarms.com

OMEGA-3 WITHOUT FISH OIL, FORTIFIED FLAX provides necessary essential fatty acids with the oil in flax seed. It is nature's richest source of Omega-3 and this ground whole flax seed also contains all essential amino acids, high fiber, complex carbohydrates, vitamins and minerals. This necessary supplement comes in meal form, and therefore is easy to mix in fruit juice or water or sprinkle on or mix into food. OMEGA-LIFE, Inc., PO Box 208, Brookfield WI 53008-0208 (800)-EAT-FLAX (328-3529)

Bibliography and Recommended Reading

Anderson, Nina and Peiper, Dr. Howard; *A.D.D., The Natural Approach*, Safe Goods Publishing, Markham, ON, 1996

Anderson, Nina and Dr. I Gerald Olarsch, N.D., *Analyzing Sports Drinks*, Safe Goods Publishing, Markham, ON, 2002

Batmanghelidj, F.; *Your Body's Many Cries for Water.*, Global Health Solutions, Falls Church, VA, 1997

Becker, Robert O., *Cross Currents*, Jeremy Tarcher, Inc., 1990.

Bell, Rachel and Peiper, Dr. Howard; *The A.D.D. and A.D.H.D. DIET!*, Safe Goods, Markham, ON 1997

Bluestone, Judy; "Not Your Ordinary Workout: HANDLE Institute Creates Unusual Exercises to Treat Attention Deficit Disorder, Autism." *Puget Sound Business Journal* (David Volk),: 23-29, May 1997

"Chronic electromagnetic frequency exposure decreases HSP70 levels and lowers cytoprotection," Journal of Cellular Biochem istry, Feb., 2002

Dennison, Paul E., PhD, and Dennison, Gail; *Brain Gym*, Edu-Kinesthetics, Ventura, CA, 1986

Gormley, James J., "PS and Other Good Fats," Vitamin Retailer, Sept., 2007

Hannaford, Carla, PhD; *Smart Moves-Why Learning Is Not All In Your Head*, Great Ocean Publishers, Arlington, VA, 1995

Levitt, Blake, Cell Towers: Wireless Convenience or Environ- mental Hazard, Safe Goods, Sheffield, MA, 2000

Mackintosh, Nicolas, Treays, Rebecca; *Understanding Your Brain*, Usborne Science for Beginners, EDC Publishing, Tulsa OK, 1996

McCord, Holly, RD, and Rao, Linda; "Top Seed with its Nutritional

Peskin, Brian, *The Hidden Story of Cancer*, Pinnacle Press, 2006

Powers, Flax is the Next Nutritional Star", *Prevention*, April 1997

McIlwain, H.; *Biochemistry and the Central Nervous System*, Boston, Little, Brown, 1959

Swarthwout, Dr. Glen; *Electromagnetic Pollution Solutions*, AERAI Publishing, Hilo, HI, 1991

West, David; Parker, Steve; *Brain Surgery for Beginners*, The Millbrook Press, Brookfield, CT, 1995

Notes

About the Authors

Nina Anderson is a nationally acclaimed researcher, author, television and radio personality. She has been an active researcher in the alternative health field for over 20 years, and has authored 18 books, including *Worse Than Global Warming: Wave Technology, Overcoming Senior Moments, 2012 Airborne Prophesy*, and *Super Nutrition For Dogs n' Cats*. Nina has a B.A. from Monmouth College, is a jet aircraft pilot and holds a Specialist in Performance Nutrition certificate from the International Sports Science Association.

Frances Meiser is an educator, author and pioneer in bringing new information on brain function and its neuroplasticity to the educational arena and an aging population. She authored *The Brain Train* and *Overcoming Senior Moments*, and is Executive Director of The Brain Train Center, a nonprofit organization that teaches "healthy habits make healthy brains." Ms. Meiser holds a Masters in Education and Early Child Development and is a frequent lecturer on brain health for both children and adults.

Susan Lee is Director of Program Development for The Brain Train Center. She earned a B.S. in Biology from the University of Houston and a masters degree in Reading and Literacy from Concordia University. She creates and teaches Brain Based Education courses for teacher certification students, and has completed numerous studies involving mind/body perfection and whole brain integration.

Other Books from
SAFE GOODS

A.D.D. The Natural Approach	$ 4.95 US
El Método Natural *(A.D.D., The Natural Approach Spanish)*	$ 6.95 US
The A.D.D. & A.D.H.D. Diet!	$10.95 US
Kids First: Health with No Interference	$16.95 US
Overcoming Senior Moments	$ 9.95 US
Cell Towers: Wireless Convenience or Environmental Hazard	$19.95 US

To order:
Safe Goods Publishing
(888) NATURE-1 (628-8731)
www.safegoodspub.com